World War One Remembered

"This, The Greatest of All Wars,
Is Not Just Another War—It is the Last War!"
H. G. Wells

To Linda—
No red pencils please.
Ⓘ

Francis A. Ianni

Paintings by Frank E. Schoonover and Gayle Porter Hoskins

World War One Remembered
by Francis A. Ianni

Copyright © 1993
Delaware Heritage Commission

A DELAWARE HERITAGE PRESS BOOK

First Printing, October 1993

ISBN: 0-924117-05-2

Library of Congress Catalog Card Number: 93-73027

The Delaware Heritage Commission
Carvel State Office Building
820 North French Street, 4th Floor
Wilmington, Delaware 19801

Delaware
• • • • • • ◆ • • • • • •
Freedom's First

Table of Contents

Cover: *How Twenty Marines Took Bouresches*
Painted by Frank E. Schoonover and restored by John R. Schoonover
Owned by the Delaware National Guard

Acknowledgment

Six of the war paintings by Gayle Porter Hoskins and nine by Frank E. Schoonover are currently on display at the Headquarters of the Delaware National Guard at First Regiment Road, Sherwood Park II, Wilmington, Delaware. Time has taken its toll on the paintings.

One of the paintings by Schoonover, "How Twenty Marines Took Bouresches," shown on the cover, has been restored by the artist's grandson, John R. Schoonover. The enhancement of the painting has caused the Delaware National Guard to explore ways to have the remaining paintings repaired and restored, and sponsors are being sought to support the project.

Appreciation is extended to the Delaware National Guard for its support of the project.

Foreword

This publication is designed to support the commemoration of the 75th Anniversary of the Armistice of World War I, November 11, 1918, by the Delaware Heritage Commission, whose major project regarding WWI will be an encampment at Fort DuPont in Delaware City, October 9, 1993. Its design is to provide a brief history of World War I and the Armistice for students and the public in general. It also depicts the war through the eyes of two Delaware artists, Frank E. Schoonover and Gayle Porter Hoskins, who prepared a series of paintings on the war, prints of which were published in color in *The Ladies' Home Journal* where they appeared in 1918 and 1919. The reproductions measured 11" by 17" and were designed to be suitable for framing as "a souvenir of the war." The effort herein is not intended to be a definitive history of the war, the artists, or the role of Delaware in the war.

My involvement in the project is due chiefly to my interest in military matters and my connection to the paintings. The first connection was a 24-volume set of books that I grew up with, ranging from nursery rhymes to such classics as *Ivanhoe, Treasure Island, Kidnapped, Robinson Crusoe, Gulliver's Travels,* and others, richly illustrated by Frank E. Schoonover. While I was essentially unaware of and unconcerned then about the illustrator, the paintings and the sense of action that they conveyed, together with the stories that they accompanied, certainly went a long way in developing my life's attitudes. I devoured these books, reading them again and again, and acquiring in the process a desire for adventure. I aspired to the attributes that they espoused: bravery, duty to God and country, respect for womanhood, and other virtues of old. I read these stories to my children, frequently inventing stories when they were too young to comprehend the pictures' full context. The well-worn books now reside with my grandchildren.

I didn't encounter a Schoonover painting again until 1977, while waiting for my confirmation hearings as Adjutant General of Delaware's National Guard in Legislative Hall in Dover. I had been called from duty in the Office of the Secretary of Defense by Governor Pierre duPont IV, to help prepare the National Guard for potential problems resulting from court ordered school bussing. On the second floor of Legislative Hall, I noticed that the portrait of Sergeant James P. Connor, Delaware's World War II Medal of Honor recipient, with whom I was familiar, had been painted by Schoonover.

After reporting for duty with the National Guard, I soon discovered in an overheated musty storeroom, collecting dust, a treasure of paintings depicting World War I scenes. I immediately recognized many of them as Schoonover's works. There were also a number painted by Gayle Porter Hoskins with whom I was unfamiliar. Shortly thereafter, the National Guard acquired the Lora Little School in Sherwood Park, and I moved the Headquarters there and converted the school library into a proper exhibition room for these dramatic paintings.

The paintings had been acquired by my predecessor, once removed, Major General Joseph C. Scannell, Adjutant General from 1950 to 1969. General Scannell had a great love for military history and travelled frequently to book fairs and sales in New York and elsewhere, acquiring old texts and prints. Over the years he had amassed an excellent military history collection all housed now in the library at the Headquarters of the Delaware National Guard.

In 1958, after learning about the paintings and expressing an interest in obtaining them, General Scannell was contacted by Arlene R. Hoskins, wife of Gayle Hoskins. General Scannell arranged for an appraisal by Leon de Valinger, State Archivist and Secretary of the State Portrait Commission. A price of $2,500 for eight paintings was agreed to and the purchase was completed on July 1, 1960.

In March, 1959, Scannell agreed with Schoonover to have nine of his paintings appraised and purchased in the same fashion, with the understanding that payment would be delayed due to the purchase of Hoskins' paintings. A price of $2,700 for the nine paintings was agreed to, with payment completed in November 1962.

Over The Top

The one phrase that captured the essence of trench warfare of World War I, the "Moment of Truth" in the terminology of the bullring, was the command, "Over The Top," the order to leave the comparative safety of the trenches and to proceed into "No-Man's Land" to face the enemy's machine guns, artillery, gas, and one's fears.

Over The Top by Gayle Porter Hoskins
Courtesy of the Delaware National Guard

A person prominent in the negotiations was Brigadier General Norman Lack, a Wilmington Trust official, who had been on Dwight D. Eisenhower's staff in England during World War II and was a friend and neighbor of Schoonover and active in veterans affairs in Delaware for several decades after World War II. The paintings were hung in the Wilmington Armory on Dupont Street until the National Guard Headquarters was moved to the new armory on Newport-Gap Pike, where they were placed in storage.

The final reason for my interest and involvement is personal. My father, Francisco Ianni, had fought in France in World War I with the 5th "Red Diamond" Division. He had arrived in Philadelphia as an immigrant on July 4, 1913, and enlisted in 1917, taking his basic training at Gettysburg where Lieutenant Colonel Eisenhower was to be assigned as a trainer. Because my father was decorated twice for bravery during the Meuse-Argonne offensive, he was assigned after the Armistice to the Honor Guard of General John J. "Blackjack" Pershing, Allied Expeditionary Force Commander, stationed first in Luxembourg and then outside of Coblenz on the Rhine River during the occupation of Germany after the war. While stationed in Germany after World War II, I visited the World War I battle sites where my father had served. When my father died, General Pershing's portrait still hung in his bedroom.

My father participated proudly in veterans affairs until his death at age 96 on March 15, 1993. His good friend, Dana Pyle, Delaware Commander and National Quartermaster and Adjutant for the Veterans of World War I, would squire him to all of these activities. He had looked forward to participation in the events at Fort DuPont. Whenever he participated in a patriotic activity, he proudly wore his Silver Star and insisted that I wear mine that had been awarded in Vietnam. Other than some of his service papers, I have only these service-affiliated mementoes of his: a shaving brush which he kept in a drawer, for which I asked when I left for West Point, intending to trim the bristles and use the brush to apply polish to the welt of my shoes. I still use it for that today. The second item was a trench knife with brass knuckles and chrome steel blade, with "1918" stamped on the handle. During World War II, my Father gave the knife to my Mother's youngest brother, PFC Anthony F. Marcozzi, who parachuted into Normandy on June 6, 1944, as a member of the 101st Airborne Division. Anthony was killed near Carentan on June 11 and is buried in the American Cemetery at St. Laurent-Sur-Mer overlooking Omaha Beach. The knife was returned with his effects and was given to me by my Grandmother when I enlisted at the age of 14 in 1945, the start of a thirty-five year military career. I wore the knife during two tours as an Infantry officer in Vietnam, and it passes on to my daughter, Marisa, who is a Captain in the Army. It is with great pride, love, and affection that I dedicate this book to the memory of my Father, and also to the memory of my Mother, Mary Marcozzi Ianni who, amongst many other things, instilled in me the love of books.

I would like to express my appreciation to Deborah Haskell, Executive Director of the Delaware Heritage Commission, for the opportunity to prepare this book. I wish I had had more time to prepare it. I would like to thank my editor, Marguerite Sheridan, who crossed my "T"s and dotted my "I"s and cut my verbiage with the verve of a cavalryman. Lynda Cook deserved a Distinguished Service Medal with Oak Leaf Cluster for displaying the skill of the best cryptologists of World War II in breaking the code of my handwriting. I would also like to extend appreciation to Jack Hawkins of New Castle for the material on World War I that he made available to me, and to John Schoonover, grandson of the artist, for his assistance. Special appreciation has to be given to Lee Ann Dean of the Delaware Art Museum who has worked on the Schoonover and Hoskins papers at the museum for a number of years, and who went out of her way to assist me, responding to every request for material and information. Without her personal support, and the support of the museum, this effort would have been much diminished.

As a final note, all views expressed in this paper are my responsibility as well as all errors and shortcomings.

Francis A. Ianni
U. S. Army, Retired
Major General

The Course of War in Europe

On the eve of the seventy-fifth anniversary of the Armistice of November 11, 1918 (the event that brought down the curtain on World War I after four years of violence such as the world has never seen), there remain only a few alive who were witnesses to the period. Only a few more, students of history for the most part, fully appreciate the significance of the names that again roll across the headlines today--Sarajevo, Bosnia, Herzegovina, and Serbia. The tug of the past seems to pull on the governments of Europe today as they pause at the brink of the black abyss of the Balkans. America, its leaders espousing again a passion for idealism, justice and freedom, urges action while the public teeters between the older tradition of isolationism and the current mantra of heroic gestures.

The First World War—called in its own time the Great War—ended the long period of peace between the armed camps in Europe as the Continent burst into flame. The spark that set it off was the assassination of the heir to the Austro-Hungarian throne by a fanatical Bosnian nationalist in Sarajevo, Bosnia, on June 28, 1914. The exact involvement of the Serbian Government was unclear but seemed implicit. Supported by the German Government which believed a localized settlement possible, the Austro-Hungarian Government sent an ultimatum to Serbia, making demands that were rejected; whereupon, Austria-Hungary declared war. When Russia, espousing support for its Slavic brothers in Serbia, ordered general mobilization (they had no plan for partial mobilization), Germany, after Russia rejected a demand that the mobilization be stopped, believed it had no recourse but to follow in kind. Germany knew it could not tolerate a fully mobilized Russia on its Eastern border, because their ability to prevail depended on first defeating France, Russia's ally, before Russia could complete its slower mobilization. Germany invaded Luxembourg on August 2, 1914, the same day of the year that Saddam Hussein invaded Kuwait seventy-five years later. The dogs of war were unleashed as the ministers and diplomats fumbled and failed to restrain them.

Before the conflict ended, other nations were to be drawn in. England, Belgium, Japan, Italy, China, the United States and others joined the Allies, while Turkey and Bulgaria joined Germany and Austria-Hungary. Europe was the center of military activity, but military campaigns were also fought in the Middle

East, Asia, Africa, and on almost every ocean. All told, about 65,000,000 men were mobilized, of whom 10,000,000 were killed. France was to lose sixteen percent of its male population, a drain that was to make the war of 1914-1918 the parent of 1940. In lives lost and wealth expended, no previous war in history approached its magnitude. Its legacy was the triumph of communism in Russia, fascism in Italy, national socialism in Germany, and World War II.

The central political and military problems in 1914 were a result of the outcome of the Franco-Prussian War of 1870 from which a victorious and united Germany arose to become the most powerful and influential continental state. Her later ambitions were to conflict with the dangerous ambitions of the Russians and Serbians. The other major powers in Europe chose sides in hopes of maintaining a balance-of-power. Germany's Chancellor, Otto von Bismarck, followed a diplomatic program aimed at peace which changed after he was asked to step down in 1890 by the new Kaiser, Wilhelm II. Pope Leo XIII, after a personal interview with the young emperor in 1888, made a statement that has been remembered ever since: "This young man is obstinate and vain, and it is to be feared that his reign will terminate in disaster."

The Balkans area, the "Powderkeg of Europe," was the focal area for conflict. A major problem was that the Ottoman Empire (basically Turkey), which controlled much of the area, was beset by decline and by revolt. Russia, often acting without reasonable caution, sought both to control the Dardanelles passage to her Black Sea ports and, under the guise of a program of Pan-Slavism, to encourage and patronize the nationalist feelings of the Slavic peoples in the Balkan provinces. In 1875 Bosnia and Herzegovina revolted against Turkey with the active support of their ethnic brothers in Serbia and Montenegro, and were later joined in the hostilities by Russia. Under a final treaty negotiated by Bismarck, Russia was stripped of some of her winnings, and Austria-Hungary received the right to "occupy and administer" the provinces of Bosnia and Herzegovina after consultation with Russia. In 1908, in response to troubles in the area, Austria exercised her prerogatives and annexed Bosnia and Herzegovina without such consultation, almost precipitating a conflict. It was this and other rivalries, together with the social and political instability of the Austrian-Hungarian Empire, that set the stage for World War I.

Even more dangerous than the diplomatic shortcomings was the failure of the major powers to appreciate the revolution in warfare caused by the impact of the Industrial Revolution. Mechanization and factory production brought about a wealth of productivity that allowed governments to spend more on their military and to maintain large standing armed forces. This brought, at the same time, pressure from their people for more democratic political institutions. New weapons were to be greatly increased in range, rapidity of fire, and lethality. The magazine rifle, the machine gun, and the quick-firing artillery piece had effectively ended the days of horse-mounted cavalry charges and tightly packed infantry formations. Earthen breastworks had been used by the Romans, and trenches were used in the American Civil War. But, when these were combined with the new weapons, hundreds could defeat thousands. Defense would dominate the offense. And, the sheer volume of firepower had superseded individual bravery on the battlefield.

At sea, all major navies, including the U.S., followed the lead of the British, who in 1906 built a revolutionary type of battleship, the H.M.S. Dreadnought, which mounted ten 12-inch guns. It had superior speed and armor, making all other classes of battleships obsolete. Even more potent, however, was the submarine or U-boat. (German for Unterseeboot, undersea boat)

The following chart shows one aspect of the dramatic changes in warfare, especially in the size of the armed forces in 1914 compared to their size in the Franco-Prussian war in 1870.

	Population (in Millions)		Per Capita Military Spending		Mobilized Army Strength	
	1870	1914	1870	1914	1870	1914
France	36.0	39.6	$2.92	$7.07	400,000	4,500,000
Germany	41.0	65.0	$1.28	$8.19	430,000	5,700,000

Germany's war plans called for a holding action against the Russians in the East and a wide turning movement in the West, the Schlieffen Plan, whose heavily weighted right wing would envelop the flanks of the French Army and attack it from the rear. To gain room to envelop on the right flank, the Germans would have to violate the neutrality of Belgium and Luxembourg. War commenced on August 2, 1914.

As the "Guns of August" barked, there was no turning back. The French, with

One Water Bottle for Forty Men by Gayle Porter Hoskins
Courtesy of the Delaware National Guard

the assistance of 600 Parisian taxicabs, were able to rush enough reinforcements to the crucial front. Paris was just barely saved (First Battle of the Marne), and the war soon settled into four years of stalemate and trench warfare, extending from the English Channel to the Alps. Gas was first used by the Germans on the Eastern Front in 1915. The English experimented with their cumbersome 27 ton tank and the French with their lighter but more useful 7 ton Renault tank. The use of aircraft, as it became more numerous and efficient, shifted from its observation role to an offensive one. Gas, tanks, and aircraft all proved useful but not decisive. In the end, the war was determined by the numbers, resources, and morale of the combatants.

It was natural for Americans to be interested in the war, and they ignored the admonition of President Wilson, in his neutrality speech of August 19, 1914, to remain "impartial in thought as well as in action." However, by September the President was asking for $100,000,000 in additional taxes and, in December, for an increase in the size of the merchant marine, and increased support for the National Guard, and training of volunteers in "the use of modern arms, the rudiments of drill and maneuver, and the maintenance and sanitation of camps...as a means of discipline which our young men will learn to value."

Troubles arose when the British interfered with full trade by ordering neutral ships into port and by placing items on the prohibited list that were not considered contraband of war under international law. Germany, unable to use its surface fleet, resorted to submarine warfare against the flow of supplies. To counter this, the British armed merchant ships, to which the Germans countered by attacking all enemy cargo ships without warning. Mistakes were bound to be made and, in 1915, the American ship *Gulflight* was attacked and the British liner *Lusitania* sunk with the loss of 1,195 lives, including 124 Americans.

Wilson protested to the British and more strongly to the Germans, who ceased unrestricted submarine warfare. As late as January 1917, President Wilson still

---

One Water Bottle for Forty Men

One of the romanticized stories of the war was an incident involving unselfishness and idealism, involving forty men cut-off from their supplies who shared one canteen, with the last man receiving more than any of the others. Each man had made himself his brother's keeper. While perhaps apocryphal, there is enough unselfishness in combat for the philosopher William James to write an essay in tribute to this unselfishness and to ask for "The Moral Equivalent of War." Hoskins received an award from the Wilmington Society of Fine Arts for this painting.

spoke of an equitable "peace among equals" and a "peace without victory." When the Allies rejected a German peace offer in early 1917, the Germans resumed their submarine attacks, causing Wilson to break off diplomatic relations. In early March, the American public was shocked by publication of an intercepted German message to the Mexican Government, the "Zimmerman Note," which proposed an alliance between Germany and Mexico to win back the latter's lost territory north of the border if the U.S. entered the war. Shortly afterwards, on the day Wilson announced that U. S. merchant ships would be armed, one ship was sunk under circumstances which permitted no excuse for error (the Germans boarded and set off bombs in the oil compartment), and four more ships were sunk in the next few days at a cost of six American lives. Worth going to war for? Wilson and others thought so. Although he campaigned in 1916 on the theme that "He Kept Us Out of War," he asked for a declaration of hostilities on April 2, and, with public opinion thoroughly aroused, Congress declared war on April 6, 1917.

The deadlock on the Western front sucked up lives at the rate of 5,000 and sometimes 50,000 a day. This deadlock, fixed by the failures of the German offensive plan and the French defensive plan, determined the future course of the war and, as a result, the terms of the peace, the shape of the interwar period, and the terms of the Second Round. In 1917, the world now looked to America. How would she respond? How would she perform? What would be the impact of her intervention?

Out of the Trenches

"The Yanks are Coming!"

One week after President Wilson gave his "Make the World Safe for Democracy" speech to Congress (April 2, 1917), asking for a declaration of war, the French launched an offensive at Arras, designed, as others had been, to provide a decisive victory. In less than a week, the French had lost 135,000 men without any significant gains. In rebellion against the futility of frontal attacks, the French "poilu," initiated the first of 119 acts of "collective indiscipline," the nightmare of mutiny, that would come close to forcing France out of the war. While it was welcome news that the "Yanks are Coming," that wouldn't occur for another 6 months to a year. To take pressure off the beleaguered French, the British launched an attack in Flanders, where "poppies grow." While suffering somewhat fewer casualties than the French, the attack had been launched after the heaviest artillery preparation of the war and the heaviest rains recorded in 30 years. The name of Passchendaele Ridge or Third Ypres with its 300,000 British casualties was to take its place along side the other hemorrhages of the war.

Later in the year, the Russian revolution knocked Russia out of the war, and another famous battle in Italy, Caporetto, was to make the position of the Allies in the West even more tenuous. Earlier, an Italian attack on the Austrians in August had been successful and seriously threatened their control of Trieste, causing the Austrians to ask for German help. A combined Austro-German force launched a surprise attack in October using a new form of offensive operations that would be refined and play a decisive role in the German offensives of 1918 on the Western Front. The new technique involved storm troopers bypassing enemy strong points. Following an artillery barrage and a gas attack that overwhelmed the totally inadequate gas masks of the Italians, the storm troopers under Major Erwin Rommel completely surprised the Italians. Totally unprepared for this mobile form of warfare, most frontline troops were surrounded, fell back, or surrendered in large numbers. This rout was memorialized by Ernest Hemingway, who was an ambulance driver during the battle, in his novel and the subsequent movie, *A Farewell To Arms*. Benito Mussolini, who had been the editor of a socialist newspaper, had served in the elite Bersaglieri on the Caporetto front as a Corporal, like a later compatriot, and was wounded by an exploding overheated cannon. He too, like the other Corporal, was to fume against the perceived incompetency of the management of the war.

One Hundred Percent Heroism, and Every Man a Yankee by Gayle Porter Hoskins
Courtesy of the Delaware National Guard

Despite the losses in the West, reinforcements were rushed to the Italian front in order to maintain pressure on the Germans. In addition to an American infantry regiment, an aviation detachment was sent that included New York Congressman (later Mayor) Fiorello LaGuardia, who had volunteered, been promoted to major and sent to Italy to train aviators. He had been trained to fly by a young New York immigrant aircraft designer and builder who had borrowed money from LaGuardia. He built parts in New York City and biked them to the end of the Long Island subway. From there he'd bike out to what later was to become Mitchell field, named after the commander of the American Air Service in France, General Billy Mitchell. Unable to repay LaGuardia, the young aircraft designer, Giuseppe Bellanca, was to later move to Delaware where he continued to design and build numerous award winning and record breaking aircraft at his plant in New Castle. After the war, his plane, the "Columbia," easily outflew "The Spirit of St. Louis," by flying non-stop to Berlin with fuel to spare only weeks after the plane had been sought by Charles Lindbergh to fly non-stop to Paris.

The collapse of morale of the French soldiers, the heavy British and Italian losses, the collapse of the Russians on the Eastern Front in 1917 put even more pressure on General Pershing to get his forces to the front line in France.

In April 1917, the Regular Army of the U. S. consisted of 133,000 enlisted men, 9,000 officers, and 67,000 National Guard troops. The Selective Service Act was passed in May and would eventually result in an Army of nearly 4,000,000 men. Due to the general level of unpreparedness, the question was raised of whether the U. S. would ever be able to put a trained force in the field in time to meet the crisis that the Allies were sure to face in the coming months.

The draft functioned smoothly, with few protests, but equipping the force was a much larger problem. Virtually all artillery, aircraft, tanks and even winter uniforms had to be furnished by the Allies.

One-Hundred-Per-Cent Heroism, and Every Man a Yankee
Hoskins, who was considered a master of depicting horses and men, captured the essence of artillery support troops operating in the rear of the trenches. Mechanization had not come to warfare in a significant way, and these troops had to be as heroic as the frontline soldiers because of the constant shelling and the occasional attack by enemy aircraft while they were in the open. With half their horses killed, the men hitched themselves to the ammo wagons and rushed them over a three mile stretch of road in time to support the attack.

Fresh from service operating along the Mexican Border against Pancho Villa, "Black Jack" Pershing was selected to head the American Expeditionary Force. He had gotten the nickname from his days commanding black soldiers. Rushing to France in May 1917 with instructions to keep the American units together, Pershing awaited his units. Regulars were organized in divisions numbered 1 to 20, the National Guard formed divisions 26 to 42, and the National Army in divisions 76 to 93, with some numbers not used.

In June, the 16th, 18th, 26th, and 28th Infantries, that were to be formed into the 1st Division in France, departed from Hoboken early in the month. In October, the Division was joined by members of the Coast Artillery Corps from along the Delaware River who had been organized at Fort DuPont into the 1st Trench Mortar Battery.

When trouble had arisen on the Mexican border in 1916, Delaware furnished two battalions of Infantry from the National Guard for service along the border. (An interesting 1916 highlight: the German Ambassador hosted a fund raiser for the Red Cross at Turner Hall in Wilmington.) The "Welcome Home" banquet held at the Hotel DuPont in February 1917 for the returning Delaware Guardsmen was the largest ever held in Wilmington. Six weeks after their return from eight months of Mexican border service, the men of the First Battalion, First Delaware Infantry Regiment, were once again called into Federal service to defend vital utility and communications points in Delaware against possible German sabotage. When war was declared in April, Delaware was authorized to raise a third battalion which was called up along with the Second Battalion.

In September the Regiment was sent to Camp McClellan, Alabama, where they froze in tents during the coldest winter in Alabama history. After attempts to use the Regiment as fillers for other units were blocked by Delaware's Congressional members, the Delaware Regiment was organized as the 59th Pioneer Infantry Regiment, retrained at Fort Dix, and sent to France in September, 1918, in time to support the attacking divisions in the Meuse-Argonne Offensive. It built and maintained roads, operated a concrete block factory, handled general construction and camouflage duties, built railroads, and constructed and operated a water supply system.

Overall, Delaware furnished 7,484 members to the Army from all sources, ranking above Hawaii, Nevada, and Alaska.

The Homefront: *The Ladies' Home Journal* "Goes to War"

President Wilson now faced the task of mobilizing the nation and organizing its war effort. Very little had been done during the thirty-two months the war had been waged in Europe to prepare either the armed forces or the nation for the challenge that lay ahead. In words of eloquent idealism, he set forth in his speech to Congress on April 2, the positive goals for which the United States should fight. It is worth reading those words against the backdrop of today's world.

> "It is a fearful thing to lead this great peaceful people into war, into the most terrible and disastrous of all wars, civilization itself seeming to be in the balance. But the right is more precious than peace, and we shall fight for the things which we have always carried nearest our hearts—for democracy...for the rights and liberties of small nations, for a universal declaration of right.... To such a task we can dedicate our lives and our fortunes everything that we are and everything that we have, with the pride of those who know that the day has come when America is privileged to spend her blood and her might for the principles that gave her birth and happiness and the peace which she has treasured.... The world must be made safe for democracy."

This last sentence above all was to be remembered by the American people from Wilson's war message.

The United States seemed to be entering the war because of the rather narrow reason that Germany had violated the country's rights of neutrality (while delivering oil to the English). Only later did the American people come to be indoctrinated with Wilson's noble aims, and also with a passionate hatred for Imperial Germany. Despite the fact that after the original English the most prominent American heritage was German, words such as "Hun, Boche, Teuton, and Prussianism" used in the form of invective, became commonplace in the most genteel company. Wilson, however, was clear to make a distinction between the German people and their government. At an increasing tempo, blaring bands, flying flags, and bombastic patriotic oratory whipped the fighting spirit of civilian America to a fever pitch. A popular song of the day was: "Just Like Washington Crossed the Delaware, General Pershing Will Cross The Rhine."

How the Government prepared the home front for war can be seen in microcosm by following the course of *The Ladies' Home Journal,* one of the nation's most popular magazines, from April 1917 through the period in 1918 and 1919 when it would print the war art of Frank E. Schoonover and Gayle Porter Hoskins. The *Ladies' Home Journal* was one of three major publications of the Curtis Publishing Company of Philadelphia, the two others being *The Saturday Evening Post* and *Gentlemen's Quarterly*. The magazine had a wide circulation, cost fifteen cents a copy (three cents of which went to delivery boys), measured 11" by 17", and ran over 100 pages per issue. In keeping with its audience, it focused, before the United States entered the war, on stories and articles of interest to women. Ads featured food, clothing, and household items. Many of the articles would be timely today. It editorialized on "The old way of the husband's doling out so much to his wife every once in a while is fast going out...no woman should allow herself to stand for it in the management of the home." One editorial in the January 1917 issue asserted: "It is said with pride that many women are proving themselves more effective than men.... But,...these selfsame women are continuing to do the work that belongs to women, and thus going beyond their strength.... There is a certain amount of work in this world that can be only women's work...." It concluded, "There are some things that are eternal!" The editors of the Journal were all men.

The February 1917 issue featured the monthly food budget of a Delawarean, a Mrs. J. Barry Baxter, for a family of five. It amounted to $50.98 and featured a weekly pint of fresh oysters each Friday during their season, a monthly cold tongue, sirloin steak at 35 cents a pound, lamb chops for the same price, veal cutlet for 25 cents, sugar at 8 cents a pound, olive oil at 75 cents a quart, and flour at 5 cents a pound, with no bread listed to be purchased. Presumably, only home baked bread would do.

Prior to April 1917 the war in Europe had been mentioned only once, a brief statement in the Editor's Comments at the opening of the January 1916 issue to the effect that the shadow of the war in Europe hung over the prospects for the New Year. In the first month after the United States declared war, the magazine opened with a hard hitting editorial. It called on all women to do their bit, "whatever-their-station." "The time has come for the American woman," it admonished, "to lay aside her dolls and playthings, as did her sister of 1861-1865." The magazine was already in touch "with the authoritative channels" on what activities needed to be undertaken and it would be their "mouthpiece and the guide of the women who wish to take part in them." An article speculated on what it would be like if we had "compulsory military training" (the draft), which came six weeks after the declaration of war (compared to the two years to get the draft enacted in England).

The shift to a "war footing" by the magazine was slow. An English Red Cross nurse was featured in the June issue, and an editorial "On Women and Patriotism" stated that "If war depended on women, there would never be a War.... The masculine mind always thinks in terms of force." In the same issue the Assistant Secretary of the Navy, Franklin D. Roosevelt, authored an article on "What the Navy Can do For Your Boy," and the first picture featuring servicemen, a Navy gun crew, was featured, followed by an illustration of Navy servicewomen serving as clerks in the Naval Reserve. The next issue featured doll cut-outs in uniform and articles cautioning against hoarding food and enemy spy techniques. An advertisement featuring Ogden Armour of the meat company of that name stated that "Unless women realize the task that confronts them, hunger and national defeat are ahead of us." William Howard Taft, Chairman of the Central Committee of the Red Cross, described the preparation of comfort kits for servicemembers, calling for two million. The Red Cross column was to become a regular feature, including regular calls for donations. Later appeals were made for the YMCA, Salvation Army, Knights of Columbus, and other organizations that provided recreation, welfare and morale support at military bases in the United States and later overseas. Gradually, the magazine had jumped on the band wagon to help prepare the populace for War.

The public response to such appeals must have been overwhelming because only a year later, the *Journal* was to report that military commanders were complaining that troops entertained in U. S. homes were being fed too much and kept up too late, and that the sending of sweets and edibles was disadvantageous to the health of the men. Commanders complained that ninety percent of social functions outside of camp consisted of dances, where the men were kept up too late and "their physical vitality impaired." Also, the "comforts" requested at the start of the war were now more than adequately being provided. Readers were chastised about writing "doleful" letters which were depressing. It concluded that the "godmother idea of women writing to the boys they do not know and whom their family pictures as being lonely—which is not true—should cease in order to stop revealed graft and corruption."

In September, 1917, the first ad appeared featuring soldiers, this one by Kodak, pointing out that soldiers wanted pictures from home. Other ads took up the military theme, and women's clothes started to feature the military look. In

At Brigade Headquarters by Frank E. Schoonover
Courtesy of the Schoonover Studios

October, when the first troop units left for France, the tempo of war related articles increased. Herbert Hoover, the Food Administrator for the United States, was introduced, urging food conservation. Articles from his agency would become a regular feature, including recipes for "War Bread" (no wheat), "Meatless Tuesday," and other means to conserving food. Major articles, such as "Men Must Not Complain If Wife Cuts Food," appeared. "Liberty Cabbage" was substituted for sauerkraut and hamburger became "Liberty Steak." Hoover's agency produced a widely distributed series of posters on canvas urging food conservation. Liberty Bonds were supported, and one canvas poster in color showed a Prussian soldier leading off a young girl and the admonition, "Remember Belgium," a tribute to the effectiveness of the British disinformation program that accused the Germans of wide-spread rape in Belgium. Sir Baden Powell, founder of the Boy Scouts, prophesied that the war would end in 1935. Did he mean 1945?

During 1918, the Department of the Interior organized the United States School Garden Army, comprised of 1,500,000 school children, to clear vacant lots under the direction of school teachers in "cities, towns, and industrial villages" to grow vegetables, using $50,000 from defense appropriations. In 1919, after the war had ended, Congress, recognizing a good thing and not ever wanting a government program to die, raised the appropriation to $200,000 and set a participation goal of 3,500,000 children.

The Journal started "The Girls Club," the "largest in the world," which was created in each state to coordinate women's activities. The masthead of the Club's column in the magazine featured a "Swastika" like symbol on each side. An article on "The Most Democratic Army," featured servicemen from twenty ethnic groups, reported on three Germans and a "Southern" Negro, but no Italian. A letter from President Wilson addressed the activities of the Knights of Columbus, reporting that thirty-five percent of the Army and fifty percent of the Navy was Catholic. This was probably done to counter rumors that are discussed later. Bryn Mawr College girls ran a "patriotic" summer vegetable farm and built a cannery. Vassar girls, not to be outdone, got up at four a.m. on their "Victory Farm." After asking what woman is going to become after the war, and pointing out that not only was an 88 year old grandmother in Italy breaking rock for the war effort and a "Women's Battalion of Death" was operating in Petrograd, it argued that the concept of "Women as the weaker sex has gone into the scrapbook."

The Dog That Saved a Regiment by Gayle Porter Hoskins
Courtesy of the Delaware National Guard

Just eight days after the declaration of war, President Wilson created the Committee of Public Information composed of the Secretary of War, the Secretary of Navy, and Mr. George Creel, civilian chairman. Creel quickly acted to give the widest possible publicity of the President's views and to garner public support for the war. A censorship policy was established and was quickly followed by congressional passage of an Espionage Act, a Sabotage Act, and a Sedition Act. Fines up to $10,000 and imprisonment up to twenty years were provided for those who printed, spoke, or spread disloyal or abusive comments about the Constitutional form of government, or for those who spread defeatism.

These policies were augmented by a force of 150,000 so called "Four Minutemen" who were sent about the country to give short speeches in support of the President's programs. Millions of copies of the President's messages, patriotic statements and pamphlets were circulated. In addition, artists and illustrators were mobilized to produce posters supporting the war effort. In response to critics of these efforts Creel, after the war, stated: "A President of the United States, in time of war, is either a *dictator* or a *traitor*, for dictatorship in war is the Constitution's direct intent."

In July 1918, George Creel included an article in the *Journal* stating that mothers were refusing to let their daughters serve with the Red Cross because of immoral conditions in France. The suggestion that several hundred nurses had to be secretly removed to a maternity hospital because they were pregnant was invented by German agents, he said.

Creel's article went on to discount other rumors. The Navy was not throwing away good food at Pacific Coast bases. The Knights of Columbus did not have a "blood oath...to wage war secretly and openly against all heretics, Protestants, and Masons." (This story had first appeared in a 1913 issue of the *Congressional Record* because it had been used in an election contest. President Wilson also wrote an article in support of the Knights of Columbus.) Also, Creel stated there

---

The Dog That Saved a Regiment

Dogs were used extensively during the war (many were German shepherds). They were frequently used to scout the battlefield, especially at night to locate wounded soldiers and to lead bearers to rescue them. They also were used as, in this case, to carry messages. A regiment, cut off from its support column, sent its dog across the gap that was covered by heavy fire. Hit by German riflemen, the collie continued to pull himself across the open ground, collapsing at the trenchline from a final bullet, his message delivered.

was "less drunkenness, less venereal disease, and better health among servicemen in France than there was in civilian life." Stories "that antagonized capital and labor, negroes and whites, and prohibitionists and their opponents" were denounced. Rumors that 200,000 coffins had been shipped to France, that stamps should be collected for their dye, and that chicken gizzards in the South should be saved, were just German jokes.

Creel's committee also published hard hitting poetry such as the following:
"My boy must never bring disgrace to his immortal sires...
I'd rather you had died at birth or not been born at all,
Than know that I had raised a son who cannot hear the call."

George Creel worked directly with President Wilson on the Information Program. After topics were created or received by his Committee, Creel would discuss them with the President. Drafts of the articles or pamphlets would be sent to the Department of State and then to the President for revision or final approval. It seems hardly credible that a head of state would be so involved in public information. But for a man who wrote all of his own speeches, encrypted and deciphered many of his most sensitive cables, and habitually composed diplomatic notes at his own typewriter, as Wilson did, it is perhaps not as astounding as it seems.

In July, Creel wrote to Frank Schoonover asking him to paint a poster for use as a colored post card by the State Department to be sent to Russian soldiers. He also did an illustration in December titled "How Liberty Came to Ivan Ivanovitch." Copies of neither, unfortunately, are in his papers. In the July 1918 issue *The Ladies' Home Journal* announced that it would henceforth run a series of "Souvenir Pictures" of the Great War, stating that all pictures had been cleared by the Committee on Public Information which enforced strict censorship. The August 1918 issue featured four souvenir pictures: Fort Dix, physical fitness training at San Diego, troops boarding a transport, and an illustration of a sailing ship named *Columbia* bearing sails with the Cross of Saville, entitled "On the Seas Once More." Its patriotic message was not clear.

The first inclusions of Schoonover and Hoskins' paintings in the *Journal* appeared in the September 1918 issue. These were two small black and white illustrations by Frank Schoonover of French aircraft attacking a German troop train and a cavalry unit. It wasn't until the November issue, the month that the war ended, that Hoskins' and Schoonover's colored reproductions of the war paintings were to appear, occupying full pages.

The degree of cooperation and the relationship between the *Journal* and George Creel's Committee on Public Information is not clear. Numerous articles by Government officials, cabinet officers and the President were, as mentioned earlier, included in the magazine. The May 1918 issue, for example, contained what was entitled "An Authoritative Announcement for the United States Government to the Women of America" with the Editor expressing his gratification that the *Journal* had been "selected as a medium by the United States Government to present this announcement to women of America."

When the *Journal* started the series that was to include the war paintings of Schoonover, Hoskins and others, the editors simply stated that they planned to do so without giving any further information as to their purpose. In a 1960 article about Hoskins in *Delaware Magazine*, in Arlene Hoskins' 1959 letter to General Scannell, and in the 1976 book, *Frank Schoonover*, by his son Cortland, mention is made that the Great War paintings were commissioned by the War Department. Whether this was true or not is unclear. No reference to this could be found in the papers of the two artists. Because the artists retained the paintings, one can only speculate that the War Department persuaded the Curtis Publishing Company to do the series and perhaps even subsided them. Also, the War Department may well have provided photographs and clothing and equipment to assist the artists in their work.

The artists' papers indicate that their material was based on ideas from both newspaper and intelligence reports. Schoonover's papers make reference to source material from the *New York Times*. Hoskins' papers include a number of

Pagari by Frank E. Schoonover
The dog, Pagari, who saved his master during a German attack (losing part of his tail in the process) visits his comrade-in-arms at the hospital.

reports from a military observer in France (possibly from the 26th Infantry, a National Guard Division from Pennsylvania), which he may have used. Hoskins, who had been a member of the Colorado Militia (forerunner of the National Guard) and was a member of the Delaware National Guard from 1917 to 1920, may have had a source of information in those organizations. The Committee on Public Information had a fairly firm policy on censorship, as will be described later, so one can only speculate that the Committee itself may have had a role in having the paintings featured in the magazine and may even have played a role in selecting the subject matter. Whatever the case, *The Ladies' Home Journal* was in fact fully involved in the creation of public opinion on the homefront.

American Expeditionary Force
Military Insignia

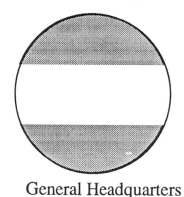

General Headquarters

First Army

Second Army

Third Army

The Artists

When *The Ladies' Home Journal* started the series on war art in color by Frank Earle Schoonover and Gayle Porter Hoskins, it represented a major commitment. Color prints had been used since the turn of the century after the development of four-color photomechanical printing. The first full color series by Howard Pyle, famous Delaware artist and teacher of both Schoonover and Hoskins, appeared in *Harper's* Christmas issue in 1900. What was unusual about the war art series was the number and the size of the pages dedicated to them. Surprising is that a womens' magazine carried art work showing themes of death and destruction, especially dead and disfigured Americans. While much in the paintings is romanticized, the paintings none the less are graphic in their portrayal of war's horror at a time when there was no clear picture of when the war would end. While all were in fact printed after the War, plans were completed in early 1918 before the Americans were fully engaged in the conflict. By comparison, no picture of a dead American serviceman appeared in print in America during World War II until 1943, nearly two years after America's entry, when the body of a dead soldier, partially buried face downward in the sand on the beach during the Pacific island invasion of Buna, was shown in *Life Magazine*. The body was in gentle repose with no aspect of the trauma associated with the death.

Before the era of color television, technicolor movies, and slick, brilliantly-colored magazines, a major vehicle for conveying visual images to the reading public was primarily through the work of magazine illustrators. Though most of the reproductions were small and printed in black and white, these artists played an important role. The pictorial images were subtle persuaders which captured readers' imaginations, enticed them to read the stories and dramatized the author's words. Improvements in photography were to reduce the role of the illustrators, but they were to continue in importance to some degree as late as 1940.

By the time of World War I, Wilmington, Delaware, had become a major center for illustrators. Felix Octavius Carr Darley (Darley Road), then enjoying his great reputation as America's first illustrator of importance, moved into his Victorian house in Claymont in 1859. He came from New York where he had illustrated Washington Irving's *Rip Van Winkle* and *The Legend of Sleepy Hollow.* He had also illustrated the works of other famous authors such as Longfellow, Harriet Beecher Stowe, Francis Parkman, and James Fenimore Cooper. Among

Frank E. Schoonover
Courtesy of the Schoonover Studios

those who had some of these illustrated books on their family shelves at that time was seven year old Howard Pyle.

Pyle was born in Wilmington in 1853 and started to attend art school in Philadelphia at the age of sixteen. Over time he developed his talents and reputation as an illustrator and artist, ranging from such early work as "Chincoteague, The Island of Ponies," to the painting, "The Battle of Bunker Hill." The latter raised questions in the mind of the viewer: "How can those men in Red march up that hill into the face of those guns?" After eighteen years of experience and a high and secure place in his field, Pyle became a teacher in Philadelphia where Schoonover became one of his first students. Later in Wilmington and Chadds Ford, Hoskins and N. C. Wyeth became enrolled.

Frank Earle Schoonover was born in New Jersey in 1877. While studying Greek through hot summer hours, preparatory to training for the Presbyterian ministry, he came across an advertisement for Pyle's class at Drexel Institute in 1896. There he was permitted to audit. Later he attended one of Pyle's summer schools at Chadds Ford, Pennsylvania. Over time he was to become one of his teacher's favorite pupils and friends.

In 1899, Schoonover moved to Wilmington where he established his first studio at 11 East 8th Street. In the following year, he moved his studio to 1305 Franklin Street where he and Stanley M. Arthurs, a Kenton, Delaware, artist, lived with Howard Pyle. Six years later he moved to his own studio at 1616 Rodney Street where he worked for the rest of his career. His grandson, John Schoonover, a professional photographer, still uses the studio as an office.

Howard Pyle was obsessed with authenticity and taught that imagination was the key to reality. That Schoonover absorbed these lessons can be seen in his papers at the Delaware Art Museum containing repeated sketches of, for example, a military canteen or the sling on a rifle as he worked to get it right. Schoonover's paintings show a mastery of action, a freeze-frame of a force of energy, typifying his lifelong conviction that "the picture must tell a strong and memorable story." It was a legend that he had a fascination for the color red, and "Schoonover Red" seemed to appear in every painting, including the red poppies on the cover of this book.

Schoonover was quite sensitive about authenticity and also criticism of this concern for authenticity. In a 1913 letter to the Editor of the *Wilmington Sunday Star*, he complained about an article, "News of the Local Art Colony," that appeared in the *Star*. "For over thirteen years," he wrote, "the school of

Gayle Porter Hoskins
Courtesy of the Schoonover Studios

illustration that is in this city has striven to give the public illustrations that ...[are] known throughout the country. It has the stamp of seriousness, individuality and originality." Schoonover criticized the "almost sacrilegious manner" used by the reporter who, in writing about a painting, "The Prodigal Son," by another local artist that had appeared in *The Ladies Home Journal*, said: "It is of the 'Parable of the Prodigal Son.' You all know about it—only the fatted calf doesn't appear in the picture, no model handy, we take it."

The response from the *Star's* manager, Joseph Martin, on stationery that identified the newspaper as "Delaware's Most Influential," and "A Metropolitan Newspaper for Delaware's Metropolis," reported that that article of the reporter ended his work for them and assured Schoonover that he and his associates "will have no reason to find fault with anything we print regarding the Wilmington artists." Were newspapers such pussycats in those days?

Schoonover did have models for his paintings, Russel Eshbach, a neighbor at his Bushkill, Pennsylvania, studio, being his favorite. "Russ," described as strapping and ruggedly picturesque with awesome vigor and strength, appeared in all fifteen of Schoonover's World War I paintings.

Schoonover was able to use in his war paintings his experience from two trips by dog sled and snowshoes to the north country of Canada, a trip to the Louisiana bayous, and a Grand Tour to Italy. Using his imagination, reinforced by photographs, articles, and whatever else available, he was able to produce paintings that are filled with action and realism, so that one can hardly believe that he had not seen war firsthand. Perhaps he was inspired by what he might have heard from his father, Brevet Colonel John Schoonover, who was Adjutant of New Jersey's Eleventh Regiment at Gettysburg during the Civil War. He had been promoted to Colonel in command of the Regiment while the battle was in progress, was wounded twice, and had his horse shot from under him. (Frank E. Schoonover did serve as an Air Raid Warden during World War II.)

Schoonover was active in the Wilmington art colony for years--teaching, as well as designing sixteen stained glass windows for Immanuel Church in Wilmington. He was a prime force behind the founding of the Delaware Art Museum. In 1972 he died at the age of 95.

Gayle Porter Hoskins, the other prominent painter who shared the spotlight with Schoonover in *The Ladies' Home Journal* World War I art series, came to Wilmington, Delaware, at the invitation of Howard Pyle at the age of twenty. He had been a mural designer for Marshall Field and Company in

Chicago. In Wilmington he established a studio at 804 Orange Street and resided at 822 Van Buren Street. Two years later he moved his studio to 1305 Franklin Street. While studying under Pyle, he lived successively in Claymont at Philadelphia Pike and Naamans Road, in Montchanin, Chadds Ford, and returned again to Wilmington in 1912. Finally, he established his studio and residence at 1625 North Rodney near Schoonover.

Perhaps best known for his exciting and scrupulously authentic portrayals of man and horse in action, Hoskins' rare ability with equine subjects came from first-hand knowledge. Born in 1887 in Brazil, Indiana, he spent most of his youth in Denver where at the age of thirteen he served as a bugler in the Colorado State Cavalry. His illustrations graced numerous magazines including *Harper's, Colliers, Red Book, The Ladies' Home Journal,* and *Saturday Evening Post.*

From 1917 to 1920 he was a member of the Delaware National Guard, and it was during this period, from 1918 to 1920, that he painted the twelve paintings that were reproduced in full color in *The Ladies Home Journal.* In later years he turned to portraiture and historical subjects. Among these were: "The Landing of the Swedes;" "Delaware's First Thanksgiving Proclamation–1778," done for the DuPont Company; "The Battle at Gettysburg," which served as the frontispiece of Stackpole's "They Met At Gettysburg;" and, in 1953, "The Battle of the Little Big Horn, June 25, 1876," done for American Heritage's "The Custer Myth." This latter painting was rather unique. Hoskins created a plaster model of the battlefield, using a U. S. Geodetic Survey Map, and had a photographer in Wilmington photograph the battlefield as it would have appeared in the lighting that existed at 4:30 in the afternoon on that day. He placed his Indians in the foreground and Custer's beleaguered remnant dimly on the ridged horizon, correcting in the process the myth created by the Anheuser Busch painting, that Custer's hair was long at the time of battle and that the manner of his end was known. Among his notable works during World War II was "The Convoy Watchdog," which depicted one of the destroyer escorts built at the time by the Dravo Corporation in Wilmington where he worked as a pattern designer.

Besides painting, Hoskins was active in the theater and co-founder of the Wilmington Drama League in 1933, over which he frequently presided. In 1925, he had joined with Schoonover to form the Wilmington Sketch Club that would later become the Wilmington Academy of Fine Art. He died in 1962 at the age of seventy-four.

The War Time Paintings of *The Ladies' Home Journal*

For the most part, the paintings of Schoonover depicted some significant military or political event. Hoskins, on the other hand, illustrated mostly human interest incidents rather than events of historical significance, and these therefore are integrated in the earlier pages of the text. Not all the war time paintings are reproduced in this text, only those where it was possible to obtain a photograph of the painting, primarily those that were sold to the Delaware National Guard. The following narrative of the war traces the conflict through the historical events depicted by the artists and covers the period after the United States entered the war. For the most part, the sections are organized in the order in which the action occurred, not the order in which they appeared in the magazine. At the time Schoonover and Hoskins were painting, they were dealing with the information at hand. In some cases, new information became available and the paintings are described in light of subsequently available information.

Coat of Arms
16th Infantry Regiment

The Greatest American Moment in the War by Gayle Porter Hoskins
Courtesy of the Delaware National Guard

Lafayette, We are Here!

To herald the arrival of American troops in France, and to celebrate the hope of the French and British people, nearly exhausted by the long year of attrition, a battalion of the 16th Infantry marched through Paris on July 4, 1917. During the parade, many women forced their way into the ranks, as Pershing recounted, draped the men and their hats and rifles with bouquets, and walked arm in arm so that "the 16th Infantry looked like a moving flower garden." The arrival of the Americans brought the hope not only of the end of the war, but an end through victory.

The ceremony began outside the tomb of Napoleon at Les Invalides, where the case holding Napoleon's sword was opened for the first time ever and the sword presented to General Pershing to hold. Instead, he kissed it. The parade led across Paris to Lafayette's grave in the Picpus Cemetery where Pershing made some extemporaneous remarks and where his friend Colonel C. E. Stanton delivered an address. There, he uttered the stirring words that caught the imagination of all: "Lafayette, we are here!" But the long arduous task of raising the fifty-five divisions that were activated, forty-two of which were to serve in France together with their support troops, lay ahead.

The build-up in the U. S. was chaotic. Plans called for six months of state side training, two months in France, followed by one month on a quiet sector in the trenches. Officers' training lasted four weeks, even less than the "ninety day wonders" of World War II. But these plans broke down under the pressure to rush troops to France after the balance-of-power had shifted toward the central powers at the end of 1917.

The training of the 1st Infantry Division was not completed until October when it was placed in the trenches on October 21, 1917. On November 3, a German raid caught it unprepared: three soldiers were killed, five wounded, and twelve captured, the first American casualties in the war.

The Greatest American Moment in the War

General Pershing's instructions from Washington were to keep the American units together. In March 1918 a crisis arose as the Germans, now outnumbering the Allies, launched their feared Spring offensive. On March 28, 1918, Pershing met with General Ferdinand Foch and declared in French: "I am here to tell you that the Americans will be proud to be engaged in the greatest battle of history. Infantry, artillery, aviation, all that we have is yours."

The Second Infantry Division followed behind the First. It was comprised of one Regular Army Brigade and a Brigade of Marines, the only other reasonably ready force available for deployment. The Marines were peeved that they had to give up their distinctive green uniform in favor of the Army khaki, but they maintained their identity by retaining Marine Corps emblems on helmets and uniforms, and by not wearing the "Indian Head" patch of the Second Division. The Marine Brigade was commanded initially by army officers until command was given to John A. Lejeune, who was to be eventually promoted to Major General and Division Commander and the only Marine to ever Command an Army Division. As the men unloaded from their transports, they were greeted by their next form of transport, the infamous "Hommes 40—Cheveaux 8," the "40 men or 8 horse" boxcars. Soon they would learn about "cooties" (body lice), "trench foot," "Over the Top," "Iron Rations," and new words such as "flak" and "ace."

The journey to Europe was not without its excitement: through the second quarter of 1917, of every four vessels that headed across the Atlantic to England or France, only three returned safely. The British fleet for the most part guarded against the German fleet. Admiral William Simms went to London to argue successfully for the adoption of the convoy system. The *U.S.S. Delaware* (BB-28), the sixth naval ship by that name, was to play a part in protecting the flow of arms to Europe.

It was the first in the line for the United States of the new heavily gunned Dreadnought class, the forerunner of the heavy battleship. Launched in 1909 at Newport News and commissioned in 1910, the ship visited Wilmington from October 3rd to 9th, 1910, to receive a gift of silver from the state and Governor Simeon Pennewill. The service, which cost $10,000, was claimed by its maker to be the most beautiful silver service ever presented to a battleship. In addition to a state flag and the silver service, large portraits of three of Delaware's naval heroes were presented to the ship: Commodore Thomas J. MacDonough, from the Delaware Society of the Colonial Dames of Delaware, Commodore Jacob Jones, from the Delaware Society of the Daughters of 1812, and Admiral Samuel Francis duPont from his niece Mrs. Eugene duPont and her son Alexis duPont. The Battleship Committee was comprised of "prominent citizens" whose names now exist on many Delaware streets, schools, and landmarks: Bayard, Heald, Lobdell, Saulsbury, Conrad, DuPont, Marvel, Hoopes, and Warner. No mention was made in the newspaper articles of the artist or artists of the portraits, but,

Howard Pyle, a noted Delaware artist, was advisor to the Committee and may have had a hand in them.

On November 25, 1917, the *Delaware* sailed to Scapa Flow, Scotland, home of the British Grand Fleet. While on escort duty to Norway, she was attacked twice by submarines. More convoy and mine laying escort duty followed, with the ship returning to Hampton Roads and then to Boston for overhaul after the Armistice. As a result of the Washington Naval treaty on the limitation of armaments, the ship was sold as scrap in 1924 and the silver service returned to Delaware.[1]

U.S.S. Delaware

---

[1]In 1978, while serving as Adjutant General, I sponsored the Olympic Torch Team's passage through Delaware as it carried the Olympic Flame to the Winter Games at Lake Placid. I borrowed the very large and elaborate punch bowl of the U.S.S. Delaware from the Division of Historical and Cultural Affairs, which required that it be kept under military guard. The bowl was placed in the Library where the paintings of Schoonover and Hoskins were on display and where a toast was given before an overflow crowd. The significance of the bowl and paintings was pointed out to the team members, and they were urged to "Go Over the Top" in medal wins and to "Sink their Opponents." In 1991, I obtained at auction an elaborate 27 inch silver tray engraved "AHB, Wardroom Mess, U.S.S. Delaware," February 15, 1913.

Cantigny: Where the Americans Won Their First Laurels by Frank E. Schoonover
Courtesy of the Delaware National Guard

Cantigny: Where the Americans Won Their First Laurels

On November 11, 1917, exactly one year before the cessation of hostilities, General Erich Ludendorff, the *defacto* commander of the German Army, summoned a conference in Belgium to plan a strike before the weight of the Americans could be brought to bear. Plans were made that were to result in five major offensives against the British and French. In March 1918 all hell broke loose as the Germans launched their first offensive to take advantage of their manpower superiority on the Western Front. Main attacks were aimed north of the American positions. As American divisions completed their training, they had been placed in the trenches under French and British Command. Aside from aggressive patrolling, no offensive operations were initiated until the end of May. The first American offensive operation was that of the 28th Infantry of the First Division against the village of Cantigny.

Villages were frequently included in the front lines and developed as strong points. While it is true that the buildings served as landmarks and offered better targets for artillery compared to a general trench line, they offered a certain modicum of comfort for the garrisoning troops despite the pounding and levelling of the well constructed homes and churches. The debris could be used for shelter, barricades were easily erected, and one could fight from the ruins of one house to the ruins of another. Such a town, when seized, upsets the defender's scheme of organization and usually jeopardizes the tenure of adjacent positions. Cantigny had been twice captured and twice recaptured before the arrival of the Americans, so the enemy had let it be known that it intended to hold the position at all cost. Thus the village of Cantigny was attacked as the first offensive operation in the War by the Americans.

Befitting the significance of the operation, it had been carefully planned by Colonel George C. Marshall, Chief of Operations for the Division, but plans were partially upset by the withdrawal of a great portion of the artillery support diverted to handle enemy attacks in adjacent areas. (Col. Marshall was to lead American forces in WWII and to become Secretary of State under another World War I veteran, Captain Harry S. Truman, commander of an artillery battery during the War.)

Accompanying the Regiment were three French tank units—one of which is depicted in the painting—a platoon of French flame thrower operators, and divisional engineers who helped with breaching and erecting barriers, and French aircraft overhead. Supporting the regiment was the 1st Battalion of the 26th Infantry under Major Theodore Roosevelt, Jr., son of the former President. (In 1944, Roosevelt was to land with the first wave of the Fourth Division at Utah Beach in Normandy and to die later in France.) Following an artillery preparation and gassing of the objective, the artillery changed to a rolling barrage starting at 6:45 a.m. The Infantry "went over the top" in three lines about 100 yards apart, with the lead line following closely upon the barrage that moved at the rate of 50 yards a minute. As the forward line neared the objective, the tanks passed through to the leading wave of the Infantry. The entire objective was reached at 7:20 a.m. on schedule. New trenches were dug and wire erected to meet the three counterattacks which came later, all of which were repulsed. The Americans took 250 German prisoners and suffered 600 casualties during the two day operation. This was a modest operation, but one that pleased both the French and Americans and no doubt caused some consternation to the Germans.[2]

---

[2] After World War II, I was assigned to Germany, serving in three regiments that all traced their lineage to World War I. The first of these was the 28th Infantry Regiment, known as "The Black Lions of Cantigny" and whose insignia portrays a black rampant lion on a white shield, the lion having been taken from the arms of Picardy, where Cantigny is located, and whose arms carry three rampant black lions. As was customary, the Regiment celebrated its organization day with a ceremony commemorating its history, reciting in detail its exploits at Cantigny along with other actions. An immense statue of a black lion stood in front of the headquarters building, and all members, while assigned to the unit, wore the French Fourragere awarded for its distinguished service in World War I.

The Regimental Commander at the time was a Colonel John Ward, who landed in 1944 with the Regiment in the first wave at Omaha Beach in Normandy. While advancing through France as a company commander, he picked up a 15 year old youth from Luxembourg who wanted to tag along with the mess detachment till the unit got to Luxembourg. The young man was, at the time of my assignment to the Regiment, with the Public Affairs and Tourism Department and suggested that the Regiment participate in some commemorative event in Luxembourg. I was sent to Luxembourg for a month to coordinate the event. While there, I tried to find the woman who had baked cakes for my Father with the sugar he had "requisitioned" from General Pershing's mess hall. While I was able to locate many landmarks my father described, I was unable to locate her. The event that was celebrated was a large parade at Ettlebruck, the first town liberated in Luxembourg in 1944 by General Patton when he swung his Third Army around to counterattack against the flank of the German attack at the Bulge. As a representative of the Regiment, I placed a wreath on the grave of General Patton in the American Cemetery in Luxembourg. Ettlebruck means Attila's Bridge, commemorating a famous battle against Attila, the first Hun, more than 1500 years earlier.

*How Twenty Marines Took Bouresches**

On May 27, the day before the testing of the 1st Division at Cantigny, the Germans had launched a major offensive against the French. By June 4, they had advanced thirty miles, capturing 60,000 prisoners and vast quantities of supplies. With Paris only fifty miles away, General Foch hurried 25 French divisions and two American Divisions, the 2nd and 3rd, toward Chateau-Thierry. Although scheduled to relieve the 1st Division near Cantigny, the 2nd was loaded into French "camions" (trucks) driven by Vietnamese drivers. (The French augmented their manpower by using people from their various colonies. Ho Chi Minh was a waiter in Paris during the war. He later petitioned the peace conferees to let the Vietnamese benefit from the Wilson's policy of self-determination.) The 2nd Division moved to a position in reserve behind a front line French division near Chateau-Thierry. The 3rd Infantry Division meanwhile was dug in on the Marne at Chateau-Thierry where its 7th Machine Gun Battalion sharply defeated all German attempts to capture the critical bridge there.

Three days after the Germans were stopped at Chateau-Thierry by the 3rd Division, the French unit in front of the 2nd Division exited through them as part of the withdrawal process (The 2nd Div. was comprised of two Army regiments and two Marine regiments). To improve their position the Americans planned a counterattack across a field of green wheat, red with poppies bobbing in the wind, on toward a hilly spire of woodland, Belleau Wood, no more than a square mile in area. These woods were full of second-growth trees and brush which concealed large boulders. Told by the French that the Germans were only in one corner of the woods, the inexperienced Americans took their word for it instead of sending out patrols.

The attack by the Marine Brigade jumped off on the 6th of June. In well-aligned waves, Marine companies crossed the field covered with wheat and poppies. Some had put poppies in their helmet straps. One company commander smoked his pipe as he waved his men forward with his swagger stick. A veteran gunnery sergeant, Dan Daly, already a recipient of two Medals of honor, led in a different style as he bellowed to his platoon, "Come on, you sons of bitches. Do you want to live forever?" The attack had commenced without an artillery preparation in order to maintain surprise. It was instead the Marines who suffered a frightful surprise as machine guns opened up on them; the Germans had three lines of defense within the woods. Despite very heavy losses, the Marines pressed

See painting on the cover.

45

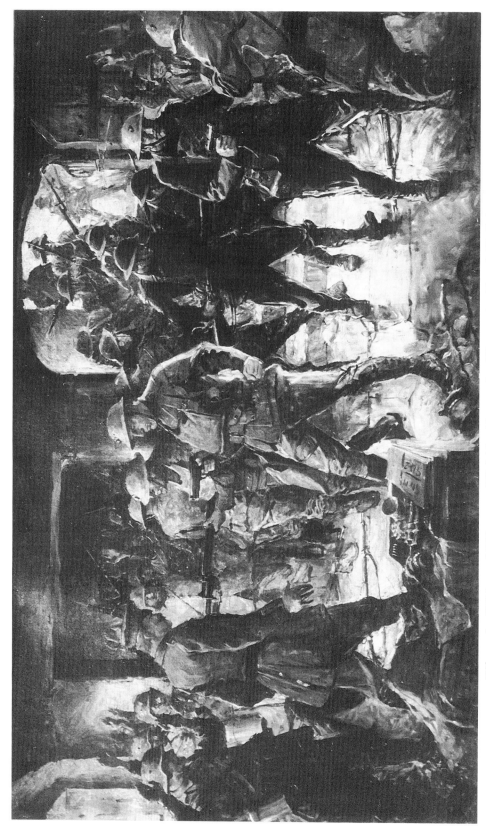

When the Whine of "Kamerad!" Lifts Above the Clamor by Frank E. Schoonover
Courtesy of the Delaware National Guard

on. Only twenty men from the 6th Marine Battalion, commanded by Major Thomas Holcomb of New Castle, Delaware, survived the assault to seize permanently the village of Bouresches. (Holcomb later became a Commandant of the Marine Corps. The Marines suffered 1087 casualties. This remained the most costly single day in Marine Corps history until twenty-five years later at the Pacific island of Tarawa.)

The Marines regrouped and attacked the adjacent fortified Bois de Belleau (Belleau Wood) for four more days against well concealed machine-gun nests. The Marines were relieved on the 15th by the 7th Infantry Regiment of the Army's 3rd Division, who were in turn relieved by the Marines on the 22nd. By the 26th, Belleau Wood was cleared at a total cost of 5,201 casualties for the Marine Brigade and a total casualty list of 8,000 since their arrival. The 2nd Division was to suffer the greatest number of casualties of all divisions in the war.

This series of actions involving the Marines caused a major flap involving the press that left a bitter taste for years afterward. The culprit was the practice of censorship which forbad the naming of any units. When a reporter asked for a clearance at American Expeditionary Force Headquarters, the regular censor was not available. As a result the newspaper headlines read: "Germans stopped at Chateau-Thierry with the help of God and A Few Marines." The net result was that the article made it appear that the Marines had saved Paris by plugging the gap on the Marne at Chateau-Thierry. But there was no gap. The Marines were not on the Marne at Chateau-Thierry; it was the 3rd Division that had stopped the Germans at Chateau-Thierry. The German advance had already been stopped before the Marines went into action at Bouresches and Belleau Wood. Besides, the 3rd Division's 7th Infantry Regiment of the Army had fought six of the twenty days involved in the capture of Belleau Wood. In fact, military critics felt that Belleau Wood should have been neutralized by gas and artillery fire rather than cleared at such heavy cost.

When the Whine of "Kamerad!" Lifts Above the Clamor

The Germans had been surprised to encounter Americans whom they had belittled in their propaganda. In the underground shelter scene depicted by Schoonover, he has again shown his attention to authenticity. In order to maintain their own identity, the Marines did not wear the 2nd Division "Indianhead" patch, instead choosing to wear their eagle, anchor, and globe crest on their helmets and uniform collars. The Germans, to indicate that they had surrendered, used the term "Kamerad."

The action at Bouresches and Belleau Woods was merely a local affair, and its result had no more than a sentimental bearing on the actual campaign. Books printed years later, however, still state that "American Marines check advance of Germans at Chateau-Thierry." And Schoonover's painting of the battle printed six months after the battle was titled: "Belleau Wood: Where the Marines stopped the Kaiser on his way to Paris," and the accompanying caption stated that the battle was one of the most crucial of the war, which of course it was not. The Marines, however, had fought gallantly. The big part the Marines played in World War I was not in Belleau Woods, but a month later in the great counterattack near Soissons. Nonetheless, in recognition of the Marines and their heavy casualties, the French ordered the name of the now famous bit of woods changed to "Bois de la Brigade de Marine." Several weeks later, Assistant Secretary of the Navy, Franklin Delano Roosevelt, visited the site. Joyce Kilmer, the poet, was killed that week.

"They Shall Not Pass!" —The Second Battle of the Marne

To meet the final German offensive, called "The Second Battle of the Marne" by the Allies, the 3rd Infantry Division was placed along the Marne River. On the night of July 14, 1918, the Germans under cover of a violent gas, smoke and artillery attack rushed to the banks of the river a great number of pontoon detachments. A counterattack checked and then pushed back the advance. Some of the combat was hand-to-hand, but Hoskins has taken some liberty in his portrayal.

The 38th Infantry Regiment's Lt. Lovejoy described the action as follows: "The 38th met every attempt with rifle and automatic-weapon fire. Scores of those boats were shattered and sunk.... Hundreds of Huns jumped into the water and were drowned. Those who reached our side by swimming were either killed or captured."

On the 15th, the 38th regiment repelled repeated crossing attempts for over fourteen hours along a front of eight and one-half miles. Since that day, the 38th Infantry Regiment has been known as "The Rock of the Marne" and the 3rd Infantry Division as "The Marne Division." (Sergeant James P. Connor, Delaware's Medal of Honor winner in World War II and whose portrait by Schoonover hangs in Legislative Hall, was a member of the 3rd Infantry Division during his service.)

"They Shall Not Pass!"— The Second Battle of the Marne by Gayle Porter Hoskins
Courtesy of the Delaware National Guard

When American Cavalry Entered the Game at St. Mihiel

Hoskins had served in a cavalry unit in the Colorado National Guard in Denver before moving to Wilmington, so it might be expected that he would look forward to painting the exploits of the cavalry. In 1914, there was more cavalry than at any time in history. The British and French had ten divisions, the Germans eleven and the Russians thirty. When the stalemate of the trenches set in, the machine gun spelled the demise of cavalry. Even in the Civil War cavalry rarely attacked, usually fighting dismounted. Cavalry was used successfully, however, in Palestine. Probably the last successful cavalry charge of history occurred during World War I at Beersheba on October 17, 1917.

Both the British and the French kept a smaller number of Cavalry divisions throughout the war to be used for exploitation if the lines were ever breached. Maintaining horses, however, was expensive. The British used more shipping space to keep their horses supplied than they used to ship ammunition to the continent.

During the offensive to reduce the St. Mihiel Salient in September 1918, Pershing had 400,000 Americans and 48,000 French in one Army for the battle. (In comparison, Grant had had about 125,000 in the Army of the Potomac. Napoleon's army at Leipzig numbered 160,000, his largest force. The Russian and Japanese Armies at Mukden in 1905, the largest engagement on record before this war, each numbered but 310,000 men.)

In July 18, 1918, two regiments of Cuirassairs, the elite of the French cavalry, made an attack through the U. S. First and Second Divisions. Madly at the charge the line swung toward the German infantry. Then began the sickening tattoo of the German machine guns, which literally cut the line to pieces. The war was to be an infantry war. Cavalry was to be used again to a much more limited extent in World War II with the same futile results.

On Friday, September 13, 1918, American Infantry at St. Mihiel had attacked over ten miles of muddy battlefield and lay down to rest. A provisional troop of the 2nd U. S. Cavalry Regiment was rushed up and ordered to cut the railroad ahead. They reached the railroad by 4 p.m. but, finding that they were not in sufficient force, they retreated. The 28th Infantry Regiment (The Black Lions of Cantigny) of the 1st Infantry Division was ordered to march through the night to

When American Cavalry Entered the Game at St. Mihiel by Gayle Porter Hoskins
Courtesy of the Delaware National Guard

cut the railroad, which they did by 10 o'clock that evening. Thus ended the one significant cavalry event of the U.S. Army. The action was not as dramatic as Hoskins had depicted.[3]

Coat of Arms
28th Infantry Regiment
(Lions of Cantigny)

---

[3] The Cavalry tradition of armies does not die easily. My last unit assignment was with the 12th Cavalry Regiment (Airmobile) in Vietnam. At Valley Forge Military Academy, I was in the last horse cavalry R.O.T.C. unit and still have the cavalry manuals we used. For parades at Valley Forge, the cavalry had to pass behind the band along a steep drop off in order to get into position to pass-in review. The band always played softly *Sambre et Meuse,* a famous French march. We dressed in the British cavalry style with spiked helmets and carried lances. At a graduation parade, the band had played extra loudly as we passed behind them, causing the horses to shy off and to slip off down the hill. After a disorganized reassembly on line to pass in review, and with the band now at the reviewing stand, the Troop Commander ordered the bugler to sound the charge. The horses needed no prodding. I felt the exhilaration of every cavalryman in history, the proud Hussars, the Bengal Lancers, the Light Brigade, the Scot Greys, Ney's Dragoons, the Uhlans, the Cossacks—it was worth my stripes. I understand Hoskins' enthusiasm for the cavalry.

The Young and Old of St. Mihiel Greet Their Liberators

The July 18, 1918, offensive to flatten the St. Mihiel Salient marked the turning point of the war. For nearly four months all German thrusts had been parried, and now the numerical superiority fell to the Allies as the tide of American arrivals swelled to its peak. Fourteen hundred Allied aircraft were massed for the offensive. The German lines got so thin as they withdrew out of the Salient that Brigadier General Douglas Mac Arthur, Commanding the 84th Infantry Brigade of the 42nd "Rainbow" Division from New York which he had created, had walked undetected on September 13 into the environs of the great fortress at Metz. Mac Arthur frequently displayed great personal courage: he was to be awarded seven Silver Stars and two Purple Hearts. By mid-September the Salient was flattened, and St. Mihiel, which had a pre-war population of 10,000, was visited on the 13th by General Pershing, celebrating his fifty-eighth birthday, while escorting Marshall Petain there. As they were leaving they encountered Secretary of War Baker and the returning citizens of the newly liberated city.

Civilians frequently occupied their villages relatively close to the front lines, tending their fields and trying to maintain as normal a life as possible, despite the casualties they suffered. Any deep thrust would force them to displace. As the tide turned, these civilians no doubt sensed that victory was near and that it was safe to venture forward to their old homes.

Schoonover, in the illustration on the following page, had painted a relatively strong looking horse pulling the farmer's wagon. This strong horse was probably in reality a much poorer animal than seen here (since the French Government repeatedly impressed horses into service) especially since horses required so much ship space. The Americans were never able to come close to supplying their own needs and had to ask the French for help.

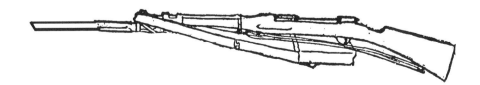

The Young and Old of St. Mihiel Greet Their Liberators by Frank E. Schoonover
Courtesy of the Delaware National Guard

Our Famous "Lost Battalion" in the Argonne Forest

By the middle of September, 1918, a succession of Allied attacks had driven the Germans back to the Hindenburg Line. With the continuing and speedy arrival of American troops during the summer of 1918, the German military leaders, Hindenburg and Ludendorff, no longer possessed the great superiority of men and guns and morale they enjoyed when they had launched their March "Victory Drive". After a year and one-half of preparation, the United States was to make its contribution: two months of extensive combat. The American role in the Fall general counter-offensive centered in the Meuse-Argonne region and started on September 26. General Pershing commanded more than 630,000 American troops and 138,000 French against 362,000 Germans. (Had this battle occurred in 1914, it would have been, in numbers involved, the greatest battle in history.) Altogether, on this day, 2,000,000 Allied troops were attacking in unison along a front of 203 miles.

During this general offensive, an event of only minor military significance occurred that captured the attention and fascination of the general public through the newspaper publicity it engendered. On October 2, after seven days of battle, the 77th Division began the assault on an entrenched and heavily wired line in the Argonne Forest. Originally, it was made up of New York men, almost entirely from the East Side or "Melting Pot" of New York City and was known as "New York's Own." Later the Division received replacements from the 40th Division from California, whose men were from all parts of the West.

The 1st Battalion of the 308th Infantry, commanded by Major Charles S. Whittlesey, and detachments from the 307th Infantry and 306th Machine Gun Battalion, received orders from the Brigade Commander to attack the heavily-entrenched German positions. At about 4 p.m., a weak spot was found in the enemy lines, and the battalion advanced to a position about a mile forward of the rest of the division, taking 90 casualties in the process. That night the Germans infiltrated behind the Battalion, cutting it off from all communication to the rear. A brigade attack by the 77th Division on the night of the 2nd and a division attack on the 4th made no progress toward relief of the battalion.

During the five day episode, the captives sent messages by carrier pigeons. "Being shelled." "20 casualties." "Casualties yesterday 8 killed, 80 wounded." "Today 1 killed, 60 wounded." "Effective strength...245." (Whittlesey had gone in with 554 men; there were 194 survivors.) A last message read: "Men are

Our Famous "Lost Battalion" in the Argonne Forest by Frank E. Schoonover
Courtesy of the Delaware National Guard

suffering from hunger and exposure and the wounded are in bad condition. Cannot support be sent at once?"

These were days of horrible hunger as well as imminent danger and death from bullets. American airplanes, reminiscent of the recent attempts in Bosnia, dropped packages of food for the men, but, in every instance, the food fell outside the lines.

On the morning of October 7, a Sergeant approached some men, stating that Major Whittlesey had asked for eight volunteers to try to get back to friendly lines, to report conditions and get rations. Led by a full-blooded Indian from Montana, this unauthorized party of nine headed for friendly lines. Eventually taken under fire, four were killed and the remaining five were wounded by a German machine gun crew and captured. Taken to the German position, Private Lovell R. Hollingshead, had the unique experience of being shown how to operate the machine gun that had been used to shoot him in the leg, followed by a firing demonstration aimed at his compatriots in the pocket. Each guide taking him to the German rear, searched him, taking nothing. Two offered to buy his Gillette razor, and one offered to trade his straight razor for it.

At the German rear, a Lieutenant Heinrich Prinz, who had been in business for six years in Spokane and spoke perfect English, interrogated him. Prinz then typed a demand for surrender, gave Hollingshead two packs of cigarettes, some bread, a cane, and a white flag, and sent him back to the battalion, emphasizing in the letter that Hollingshead had refused to divulge any military information. Whittlesey, shown wearing glasses in the painting, eventually was able to get a messenger back to friendly lines, and a rescue force broke through to relieve the unit. Whittlesey and two other officers were awarded Medals of Honor for the valiant defense.

The episode, an occasion for pride by all who had participated, was not without its tragedy. "Buck Private" T. C. McCollum from Ohio, kept alive the memory of the event by publishing five collections of rhymes, poems, essays, articles, and testimonials of the Battalion's history. After attending the interment of the Unknown Soldier at Arlington Cemetery on April 11, 1921, with other Medal of Honor recipients, Major (then Lieutenant Colonel) Whittlesey committed suicide on November 29. McCollum's records mention some of the resentment that some members felt about the publicity they had received, the bitterness aimed particularly at the press after Whittlesey's suicide. "A leading New York newspaper," wrote one officer, "that should have known better, since a score of its pre-war staff were officers in the 77th Division, suggested the other day that Lieutenant Colonel Whittlesey might have been driven to suicide through a feeling of guilt for having led the "Lost Battalion, into a trap in the Argonne...." The writer went on to say that all America was misinformed not only concerning Whittlesey, but practically everything else that took place in the A.E.F. (American Expeditionary Force)."

Resenting the allegation that the Battalion was "lost," a sentence from the order sending the Battalion into the attack was quoted: "The general says you are to advance behind the barrage regardless of losses." Whittlesey, the lawyer-soldier, it was argued, led his men to where they were because he was ordered to, and their predicament resulted from the inability of units on their flanks to make advances equal to his.

Published accounts in 1918, reported in apocryphal language that Whittlesey had responded "Go to Hell" when summoned by a German officer to surrender. This was denied in the unit's accounts, the reports denounced as "fustian and claptrap which so wins the gallery," all reminiscent of McAuliffe's "NUTS" at Bastogne in World War II and General Cambronne as reported by Victor Hugo in his response given to the British demand for Napoleon's Imperial Guard to surrender at Waterloo: "*Merde!* The Guard dies, it does not surrender." An article that appeared in the *American Legion Weekly* stated that most accounts of the incident "were fanciful, based on stories told by self-nominated heroes or by artists in words who were not there."

"Buck Private" McCollum, the Battalion's unofficial historian, had negotiated in 1928 with Schoonover for the purchase of the painting and with *The Ladies' Home Journal* for reproduction of the painting. Schoonover apparently had worked from journalistic accounts after the event. His version depicted the moment a German request for capitulation arrived at the beleaguered "Lost Battalion's" position, where they were surrounded by enemy forces for five days. McCollum eventually declined to purchase the painting because "The message of surrender was delivered by an American soldier, whereas your painting depicts a German prisoner. Fully appreciative that at the time this subject was made that undoubtedly the facts of the Lost Battalion were considerably garbled and the reproduction was only quite naturally your impression at the time."

The unit that was ordered to link up with the "Lost Battalion" was the 82nd Division (later to become the 82nd Airborne Divison). The attack order was written by Lieutenant Colonel Jonathan M. Wainwright (later of Bataan and

Corregidor fame). During the attack, a corporal in the 328th Infantry Regiment of the 82nd Division, Alvin C. York, who, despite his religious objection to war, had been drafted, single-handedly routed a German battalion. He captured 132 prisoners, 32 machine guns and killed at least 28 Germans. It would be sometime before York's exploits would become known to the public and be captured on canvas by Schoonover.

Another unit that participated in the offensive adjacent to the "Lost Battalion" was the 92nd Division, comprised of blacks but whose officers at the upper echelons were non-blacks. Another black Division, the 93rd, had its battalions parcelled out to the French where they performed with distinction. Blacks were also represented in the non-divisional units of the Army. In all, 367,000 served in the Army, 5,328 in the Navy, and none in the Marines. Their experience differed little from their experience in society. Despite President Wilson's plea that this was a war to preserve democracy, prejudice was to prevail. Pershing had served as commander of a black unit in Haiti and expressed the belief that black units performed best with white officers. President Wilson, despite his liberal democratic views, felt that black soldiers returning from abroad would be the greatest medium for conveying Bolshevism (Communism) to America. The French, he said, had treated them on an equal basis, and "It had gone to their heads." Forgotten were the medal winners and outstanding units while the actions of poor units were exaggerated. It wasn't until thirty years later that a World War I veteran, President Harry S. Truman, took steps to fully integrate blacks into the Armed Forces.

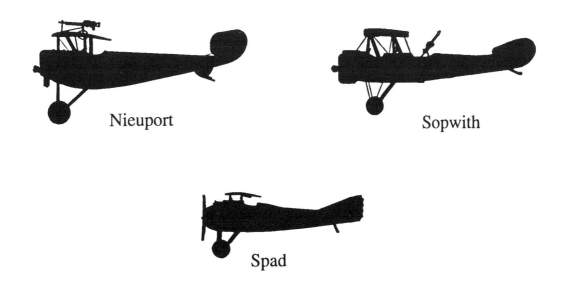

Nieuport

Sopwith

Spad

Contact by Frank E. Schoonover
Courtesy of Eleanor Foster

The War in the Air

Aviation was only fourteen years old when the United States entered the war, but aircraft had improved dramatically due to the War's impetus. The number of aircraft and aerial techniques was increasing so rapidly, that aircraft were on the verge of becoming a major tool for destruction and terror. Aviators had replaced the knights and cavalrymen of romantic novels, observing what little chivalry was to be found in battle. They provided most of the glamorous heroes of the war, much to the disgust of those unsung heroes wallowing in the mire of the trenches.

It was not without irony that a ground officer wrote: "Every whim of the ace flier was law to the ground force of the flying field which had 'My Lord's' steed ready for him to mount before he rode forth to the tournament of the skies. Aces had their names emblazoned in communiques, while the surviving officer of a veteran battalion which took its objective was not mentioned. Ascending, well-groomed and well-fed, to death in a plane seemed much more pleasant than going over the top from filthy trenches, to be mashed up in No Man's Land among putrid corpses." The doughboy, he felt, got no respect.

To the doughboy, aerial combat overhead took on aspects of a Nero circus. And the airmen, enjoying what to them was a modern day jousting tournament, displayed exuberance and overconfidence. One American pilot fell out of his airplane because he had failed to buckle himself in. And when Colonel Mitchell's pilots were forbidden to date American nurses in a nearby hospital because they brought the nurses back so late, they flew a large formation over the hospital, festooning it and its environs with long ribbons of unrolling toilet paper. They were to become more sober when the deaths started to pile up. Among these was the death of Quentin Roosevelt, a pilot and son of the former President.

Romance aside, the Air Service, however, was a disappointment to the American people because it did not, as they had hoped, produce a break in the stalemate. General George Squier, head of the Army aviation section, had evoked in congressional hearings images of "winged cavalry sweeping across the German lines and smothering their trenches with a storm of lead." "The road to Berlin lies through the air," he said. The public had hoped too much and had been promised too much, and then had been angered by the fiascoes that occurred in production in the United States. Numerous instances of wastage had occurred, and development and production were far behind those of England, France, and Italy, despite the lead that the Wright brothers had given us.

Taking Off by Frank E. Schoonover
Courtesy of Michael D. Goldman

Colonel William Mitchell, the American aviation enthusiast, had recommended that 4,500 airplanes be sent to France in 1918, with 2,000 airplanes and 4,000 engines to be manufactured each month. Caught up in the enthusiasm, Congress, urged on by the press, appropriated $639,000,000. Mismanagement of the program however was rampant. In the end, the American Expeditionary Force (AEF) obtained almost no satisfactory planes from the United States. Despite this fiasco, America did produce enough superior aviators using British and French planes who were to operate under the control of Colonel (later Brigadier General) Billy Mitchell.

Mitchell was able to use as a cadre many American pilots who had flown as volunteers with the British and especially with the French Lafayette Escadrille. One of these pilots was the first black combat aviator, Eugene "Jaques" Bullard, a decorated and wounded veteran of the French Foreign Legion. When the U. S. Army invited the pilots of the Escadrille to join the U. S. Air Service, the invitation was not extended to Bullard.

Mitchell was able to build on the flying experience of these pilots and the Allies' operational experience. Aircraft were used for bombing and strafing behind the German lines, disrupting enemy supply lines and weakening troop morale. Pilots checked on both German and friendly troop movements, dropped messages to out-of-contact or isolated units, engaged especially in "dog fights" with German Air Patrols, and shot down German observation balloons while protecting their own. American observers in balloons became so good at parachuting to safety when they came under attack that, although they jumped 116 times, only one man was killed.

Because of the new air dimension, ground troops had to pay more attention to camouflage and to restrict most movements until nightfall. Anti-aircraft units had to be deployed, and both sides started to mass their aircraft to support major ground efforts. By September, 1918, when the Americans began the St. Mihiel offensive, Mitchell had over fourteen hundred aircraft under his command. At the Armistice, General Mitchell viewed with satisfaction the overall achievements of the Air Service: his pilots had shot down 927 German airplanes and balloons while losing only 316, a ratio of three to one. Overall, Allied air efforts had mostly served to balance out those of the Central Powers.

The Ladies' Home Journal did not feature the exploits of the American pilots, relying instead on paintings by a French Officer, Lieutenant Henri Farré. One pilot featured by Farré was the legendary French air ace, Georges Guynemer.

Bombing by Frank E. Schoonover
Courtesy of Eleanor Foster

(Schoonover was to do two black and white illustrations about Guynemer for the *Journal*.) This fragile youth, suffering possibly from TB, shot down 53 Germans, including one quadruple victory and several triples. This self-proclaimed "killer of Germans," was wounded twice and shot down eight times. He disappeared during the Battle of Flanders. The National Assembly and Senate enshrined Captain Guynemer in the Pantheon as "embodiment of France's will to endure despite her grave wounds." An oft repeated tale about Guynemer involved an incident where he noticed that his adversary's gun had jammed. He waved farewell and broke off flight, leaving his opponent (the source of this account), six victory German ace Ernst Udelt, so stunned and then disturbed that he had to take extended leave. Militarily speaking, Guynemer's gesture proved absurd. Udelt later shot down 52 more Allied aircraft, became Germany's second-highest-scoring ace, and survived the war.

Another French ace (45 victories), Charles Nongesser, could count nearly as many wartime injuries: a fractured skull, shattered right arm and palate, broken jaw (seven times) and legs, dislocated knees, clavicle, left wrist and right foot. After the war he flew in Cuba and the United States in exhibitions and movies. On May 8, 1927, he took off in his plane "l'Oiseau Blanc" (White Bird) from LeBourget to fly the Atlantic nonstop. He disappeared without a trace. Had he succeeded, he would have beaten Lindbergh by 12 days.

Many pilots of this period were to gain extended notoriety or prominence in the next war. Captain Eddie Rickenbacker, went from auto racing to chauffeuring General Pershing to flying where he became America's top Ace with 26 kills, and then to Eastern Airlines. Captain Hermann Goering who was to head the Luftwaffe in World War II, took over the squadron of Manfred von Richthofen, the "Red Baron," who was Germany's leading Ace. The Red Baron had 80 kills before his death.

Mitchell went on to champion air power, especially the need for an independent air arm designed for heavy bombardment. Long-range bombardment had been tried during the War, especially by the British, but only in a limited way. President Wilson was specifically opposed to air attacks beyond the battlefield. Raynol Bolling, who was to become deputy of the U. S. Air Service in France, had been sent to Italy to observe their air arm in action. There he saw the work of Gianni Caproni, who had designed the only strategic bomber available to the Allies, and Colonel Giulio Douhet, the famous airpower theorist, who was relieved of the command of his aviation battalion for exceeding his authority on

The Hit by Frank E. Schoonover
Courtesy of Schoonover Studios

the General Staff in authorizing construction of the bomber. Caproni and Douhet continued to agitate for an Allied fleet of strategic bombers (Douhet from prison for having left a paper on a train that criticized the government). Bolling's report had high praise for the long-range bombing concept he observed and carried this message of the offensive use of bombers advocated by Caproni and Douhet which he repeated upon his assignment to France. Bolling was to be killed later on the ground when he stumbled into the advancing Germans, killing several before he died. (Bolling Air Force Base in Washington, D.C., was named in his honor.)

While Mitchell had advocated tactical air operations during the War, he later shifted his thinking in the direction of Bolling's report and Caproni and Douhet's long range bombing theories. He eventually challenged the Navy with his views of the role of long-range bombers and the Army on the need for an independent air arm. He turned out to be wrong about bombers dominating navies (It was carriers and their aircraft that did that.), but the importance of air power and an independent air arm were to prove true, but not without some significant consequences.

The airmen in France chafed from Pershing's recommendation that increased rank and pay for men engaged in flying be abolished, the placement of men who were not fliers (and not always cordial) in top command of the Air Service, and a desire for a more centralized air effort. These and other issues were not to be fully resolved until after some bitter lessons in World War II. Eisenhower granted full independence to the Air Corps in Africa in WWII after the rout of the U. S. Army II Corps at Kasserine Pass. The Corps Commander, Major General Lloyd Fredendall, whose headquarters before shipping out for the North African Invasion was at the Wilmington Armory, was replaced by General Patton. The Air Corps had never had its heart in close air support, and under the new air organization, emphasized intermediate and long range air operations. As a result, when Patton invaded Sicily, he did not know what the air plan was, and General Bradley had to escape from the beach in a DUKW amphibious vehicle when a German counterattack reached the beaches and no close air support was available. D-Day in Normandy presented the same problem. Of the 25,000 air sorties flown on that day, only 11 were close air support missions. The gap between the airmen and soldiers was shown again when bombers under the command of General Brereton (a pilot in WWI) dropped bombs on American troops in France at St. Lo, killing among others, General McNair (Ft. McNair, Wash., D.C.) because Brereton didn't inform the ground force of his plans and wouldn't permit air-ground communications at St. Lo. The air-ground coordination issue was only resolved when air controllers were put in Patton's tanks when he led his Third Army in the breakout from the beaches in France.

The U. S. was hindered in its strategic bombing campaign by the limitations of the "Flying Fortress" and the "Precision Day-Light Bombing" concept (10 good airmen went down with each plane–raids on Berlin killed 10,000 Germans at the price of 10,000 airmen) until the development of a long-range fighter escort, the P-47. The lessons learned about air power in World War I were to be unevenly translated to World War II.

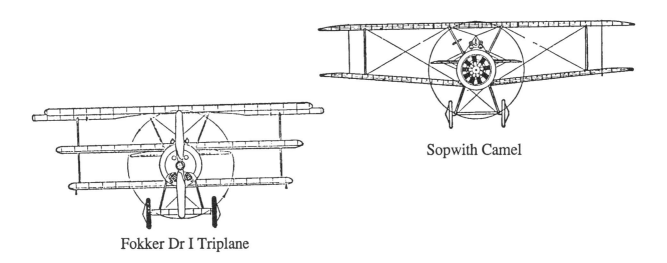

Sopwith Camel

Fokker Dr I Triplane

The "Victorious Retreat" Back to the Rhine

At the end of September 1918 the Allies launched the final offensive that was to end the war. By late October and early November the German Army was in retreat across the entire front. Stiff resistance was still to be found, and the Allies for the most part pressed forward resolutely. Schoonover's portrayal of roads choked with lumbering army transports and huge cannons and desperate men seeking relief from the scores of fighting and bombing planes, paints a grim picture of a defeated Army being pummeled to death. The planes appear to swarm like messengers of death, ceaselessly showering destruction upon the struggling men. A similar picture of the Iraqi column carrying the loot out of Kuwait hit by U. S. fighter-bombers in Desert Storm produced sufficient cries of "massacre" to induce an early termination of the war thereby permitting much of the Republican Guard to effect an escape. (In all, only forty-six bodies were amidst the debris of the Iraqi column. Most had simply escaped into the desert on foot.)

The "Victorious Retreat" Back to the Rhine by Frank E. Schoonover
Courtesy of the Delaware Art Museum

Under the White Flag by Frank E. Schoonover
Courtesy of the Delaware National Guard

Under the White Flag

When the last German offensive had failed in August 1918, a tentative decision to seek terms was made, but the German Government took no action. On September 29, Ludendorff informed the Emperor that they could not win and advised him to contact President Wilson, who had announced his *Fourteen Points for Peace* in early January. Besides the deteriorating military situation and the lack of reserves, the home front was collapsing with rioting, anarchy, mutiny, and revolution at hand. The vacant Chancellorship was thrust on Prince Max of Baden who sent a message to President Wilson requesting an immediate Armistice. The President's reply was sent without consultation with the Allies, a fatal flaw, that he was to repeat later. It was also an election year, and the Republicans were clamoring for unconditional surrender as opposed to Wilson's Fourteen Points. In the end the Allies agreed to let the military advisors set the terms of the Armistice, which ended up as unconditional. Progress was possible after the Kaiser renounced his throne and went into exile in Holland.

Schoonover caught the moment of the arrival of the German armistice delegation on November 7 at the French lines at La Capelle at 10 o'clock at night preceded by a bugler from the Uhlans, the German cavalry, who blew a bugle as the party crossed no-man's land, to announce the presence of the group which had been much delayed until darkness by the chaos on the roads in the German rear. Matthias Ergberger, a Deputy in the Reichstag and head of the Armistice party, holds his brief as head of the delegation. Major General von Winterfeldt, who spoke perfect French, is to his left; and Captain Vanselow, representing the Navy, is in the second car. Hindenberg would not permit a German Army representative to attend. He thought this would create the illusion that the Army had not been defeated and was not surrendering. This foreshadowed a problem for the future. Meeting in General Foch's railway dining car on the next day in the Forest of Compiegne, the Armistice was eventually signed at 5:00 a.m. on Monday, the 11th, to go into effect on the 1,568th day of the war, "At the Eleventh Hour of the Eleventh Day of the Eleventh Month."

As the news spread, both sides fired the cannons up to the last moment and beyond. In the European capitals, there was widespread jubilation while Americans were asleep as the news arrived. The Great War was over, but the peace was not secured. In Berlin, Premier Ebert reviewed the homecoming troops day after day from a rostrum opposite the French Embassy before crowds cheering and waving handkerchiefs. "No enemy overcame you," he said. "You protected the land from invasion.... You can return with heads erect." A myth, "The Stab in the Back" legend was born and nourished for future use. The harsh peace terms and high reparations resulted in runaway inflation together with resentment of the War Guilt clause of the peace treaty, which ascribed all fault to Germany. This contributed along with the threat of Bolshevism to the rise of Hitler. (Twenty-two years later, Hitler would do a jig at the site of the railway car as his armistice terms were read to the vanquished French. The car was then moved to the German Chancellery in Berlin where it was destroyed by Allied bombing in 1943.) At home Wilson was criticized for failing to take Congress and the public into confidence about its peace plans. The *Washington Post* reported that "for good or ill, President Wilson leaves for Europe without the united support of the American people." The Allied soldiers had won the war, but their political masters showed no such capacity to win a peace.

When Pope Benedict Greeted President Wilson

After the end of the War, President Wilson went on a tour of the capitals of the Allies in Europe. During his visit to Italy, he met with Pope Gregory XV on January 4, 1919, in Clementine Hall in the Vatican. This scene captures the moment when Monsignor Tacci, Major-Domo, escorted the President into the room as twenty-four Swiss Guards in multi-colored uniforms designed by Raphael present arms with their halberds. After the Pope and the President spoke for twenty-minutes, the Pope presented a mosaic of Guido Reni's famous picture of St. Peter to the President. Schoonover had studied in Rome in 1907, and his son, Cortland, later wrote that there he had received his most artistic stimulation.

When Pope Benedict Greeted President Wilson by Frank E. Schoonover
Courtesy of the Delaware National Guard

Doughboys First by Frank E. Schoonover
Courtesy of the Delaware National Guard

Doughboys First

Following the Armistice, the units of the American Expeditionary Force started the two-hundred mile trek to Coblenz where they were to occupy one of the three Allied bridgeheads across the Rhine River at the point where the Moselle River joins it.

Leading the way was the 1st Infantry Division, with its four Regular Infantry Regiments and the 1st Trench Mortar Battery with soldiers from Fort DuPont, Delaware. "First in France, First in Paris, First in line, First to open fire, First to suffer casualties, First to capture prisoners, First to raid, First to be raided, First in length of time spent in the front line, First in Germany, but--last to leave." It returned from France with General Pershing and marched behind him in the great victory parades of New York City and Washington, D.C.

Schoonover depicted the moment the Division crossed the Moselle River to enter Germany, and where the Division Commander General Frank Parker stepped aside to let the Infantrymen of the 16th Infantry Regiment be the first to enter Germany. (They had been the first to land in France and march through Paris on July 4, 1917.)

After the war, General MacArthur wrote a tribute to the American Doughboy, especially the Infantryman, who had borne the brunt of the War.

> "Blue-lipped, smudged with sludge, chilled by the mud and the rain of his fox hole, forming grimly and without emotion in the murk which the ground was throwing up, as heavy as that which the skies were letting down, he drove through to his objective with a dash, a ferocity and a power that his normal placidity and good nature had belied. During these moments he was transformed. Alertness, initiative and dash overcame weariness and all the tests to which his endurance had been subjected. He would not be stopped; and if the moment offered any advantage which he could gain, he would seize it, under his officers if they were present, by his own ends if they were not. He has written his history in letters of red on his enemy's breast and no man can add to it. But when I think of his patience under adversity, his fortitude under suffering, his resolution under danger, and his modesty under victory, I am filled with an emotion that I cannot trust myself to express. Crusader that he was, he kept the faith unto death that a nation might live to fulfill its destiny."

These words provide an appropriate ending to the narrative and pictorial tribute to the Americans who fought in this Great War. America had given 50,000 of her sons. Delaware had given 244. America may have come late, but she had come in time.

Coat of Arms
38th Infantry Regiment
(Rock of the Marne)

When Peace Came: The King of the Belgians Went Home
On August 2, 1914, the Germans, in violation of neutrality treaties, demanded free passage through Belgium so they could execute an envelopment of the French Army. King Albert with the support of his parliament refused, and he led his army against onrushing Germans. Forced to retreat, he fought on in France for four years. In 1918 he led his victorious soldiers back into Bruges on October 19 as a hero to the Belgian people.

When Peace Came: The King of the Belgians Went Home by Frank E. Schoonover
Courtesy of the Delaware National Guard

Illustrations

Bibliography

Braim, Paul F. *The Test of Battle*, Dissertation. Newark, Del.:University of Del., 1983.

Brook-Shepherd, Gordon. *November 1918*. Boston: Little, Brown & Company, 1918.

Bruntz, George G. *Allied Propaganda and the Collapse of the German Empire in 1918*. New York: Arno Press, 1972.

Coffman, Edward M. *The War to End All Wars*. New York: Oxford Univ. Press, 1968.

Cornebise, Alfred E. *War As Advertised*. Philadelphia: The American Philosophical Society.

Department of the Army. *American Military History*. Washington, D.C.: U. S. Government Printing Office, 1959.

Devine, Donn. *Delaware National Guard*. Wilmington, Del. 1968.

Ferrell, Robert H. *Woodrow Wilson and World War I*. New York: Harper & Row, 1985.

Freidel, Frank. *Over There*. Boston: Little, Brown and Company, 1964.

Gale, Oliver M. *Americanism: Woodrow Wilson's Speeches on the War*. Chicago: The Baldwin Syndicate, 1918.

Griess, Thomas E. *The Great War*. Wayne, N.J.: Avery Publishing Group, Inc., 1986.

Halsey, Frances Whiting. *The Literary Digest, History of the World War,* Volume VI. New York: Funk & Wagnalls Co., 1919.

Harbord, Major General James G. *The American Army in France*. Boston: Little, Brown and Co., 1936.

Harper's Pictorial Library of the World War. Vol. V, The United States in the War. New York, 1920.

Hoskins Papers, Delaware Art Museum. Wilmington, Delaware.

Jones, Barbara. *Popular Arts of the First World War*. New York: McGraw-Hill Book Co., 1972.

The Ladies' Home Journal. Philadelphia: Curtis Publishing Company. 1914-1920.

Leonard, Arthur Roy. *War Addresses of Woodrow Wilson*. Boston: Ginn and Company, 1922.

Macksey, Kenneth. *Rommel: Battles and Campaigns*. London: Mayflower Books, Inc., 1979.

Means, Mary C. *Negro Officers in the First World War*. (Thesis) University of Delaware, 1977.

The Meuse-Argonne Battlefield. Clermont-Ferrand, France: Michelin & Co. 1920.

Mitchell, William B. *Memoirs of World War I*. New York: Random House, 1960.

Morrow, John H., Jr. *The Great War in the Air*. Washington: Smithsonian Institution Press, 1993.

Pitz, Henry C. *The Brandywine Tradition*. New York: Weathervane Books, 1968.

Preliminary History of the Armistice. Carnegie Endowment for International Peace. New York: Oxford Univ. Press, 1924.

Ropp, Theodore. *War in the Modern World*. New York: Duke Univ. Press, 1959.

Schoonover, Cortland. *Frank Schoonover*. New York: Watson-Guptill Publications, 1976.

Schoonover Papers. Delaware Art Museum. Wilmington, Delaware.

Society of the First Division. *History of the First Division During The World War*. Philadelphia: The John C. Winston Co., 1922.

Stamps, Col. T. Dodson and Esposito, Col. Vincent J. *A Short History of World War I*. West Point, N.Y.: U. S. Military Academy Adjutant General Printing Office,1950.

Taylor, A.J.P. *The Origins of the Second World War*. Greenwich, Conn.: Fawcett Publications, Inc., 1961.

Tuchman, Barbara. *The Guns of August*. New York: Dell Publishing Co., Inc., 1962.

Terraine, John. *To Win a War*. New York: Doubleday & Company, Inc., 1981.